One cannot have too large a party.
-Jane Austen

Jalapeño Poppers

24 pickled jalapeño peppers
1 lb. Cheddar cheese
1/2 c. cornmeal
1/2 c. all-purpose flour

1 t. salt
2 eggs, beaten
oil for deep frying

Make a short slit into each jalapeño pepper; remove as many seeds as possible. Slice cheese into strips 1/4-inch wide and one-inch long; lay one in each jalapeño. Combine cornmeal, flour and salt in a small mixing bowl; place beaten eggs in a separate bowl. Dip peppers into egg mixture, then roll in cornmeal mixture until well coated. Set aside on a wire rack for 30 minutes; deep fry in 375-degree oil in small batches until crisp and golden, about 4 minutes. Remove using a slotted spoon; drain on paper towels. Makes 2 dozen.

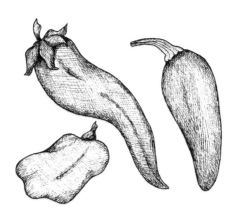

For a milder or kid-friendly version of this favorite, just use banana peppers instead of jalapeños!

Sour Cream-Ham Dip

1 c. sour cream
1/2 c. mayonnaise
1/4 t. Worcestershire sauce
1/2 t. garlic salt

1/8 t. pepper
1 c. cooked ham, finely
   chopped

Combine all ingredients; chill one hour before serving. Serve with potato chips or onion crackers. Makes 2-1/2 cups.

Oven-Toasted Potato Chips

1 lb. new potatoes, sliced
   1/8-inch thick

2 T. olive oil
1 t. salt, divided

Rinse sliced potatoes with very cold water; pat dry. Toss in oil and 1/2 teaspoon salt. Spread in a single layer on an ungreased baking sheet. Toast at 500 degrees for 20 to 25 minutes, until golden brown. Sprinkle with remaining salt; serve warm. Makes one pound.

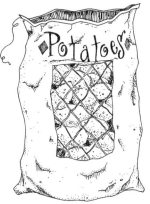

Make Oven-Toasted Potato Chips with a little more kick...sprinkle with Cajun or barbecue seasoning!

South Street Tortilla Roll-Ups

8-oz. pkg. cream cheese,
 softened
1 onion, chopped
8-oz. container sour cream
1-1/4 oz. pkg. taco
 seasoning
8-oz. pkg. shredded Cheddar
 cheese

4-1/2 oz. can diced green
 chilies
2 tomatoes, chopped
hot pepper sauce to taste
10 8-inch flour tortillas
Garnish: salsa and
 guacamole

Combine cream cheese, onion, sour cream and taco seasoning; stir until smooth. Fold in cheese, chilies, tomatoes and hot sauce, blending well. Spread mixture on tortillas, then roll tortillas. For easier cutting, refrigerate roll-ups until cream cheese mixture is firm. Slice into one-inch pieces; serve cold with salsa and guacamole. Makes 5 to 6 dozen.

A vintage tin picnic basket is a fun way to take
an appetizer to a picnic gathering.

Crescent Chicken Bites

8-oz. tube refrigerated
    crescent rolls
3-oz. pkg. cream cheese,
    softened
4 T. margarine, melted and
    divided
2 c. chicken, cooked
    and cubed

1/4 t. salt
1/8 t. pepper
2 T. onion, chopped
2 c. seasoned croutons,
    crushed

Separate crescent rolls into 4 rectangles; seal perforations and set aside. Blend cream cheese and 2 tablespoons margarine until smooth. Add next 4 ingredients; mix well. Spoon 1/2 cup chicken mixture into center of each rectangle; pull corners of dough to center of mixture and seal. Brush tops with remaining margarine. Sprinkle with crushed croutons. Bake on an ungreased baking sheet at 350 degrees for 20 to 25 minutes or until golden. Slice in half before serving. Makes 8 servings.

Tasty tidbits that are ready in no time! Softened cream cheese is delicious piped into hollowed-out cherry tomatoes, pea pods or celery sticks.

Tropical Chicken Wings

2 to 3 lbs. chicken wings
10-oz. bottle soy sauce
46-oz. can pineapple juice

5 cloves garlic, chopped
1 to 2 t. ground ginger
1 c. brown sugar, packed

Parboil chicken for 20 minutes. Combine remaining ingredients in a large bowl; add chicken. Cover and refrigerate 2 to 3 days. Place mixture and chicken in an ungreased 13"x9" baking dish. Bake at 400 degrees for 5 minutes, turn wings and bake 5 additional minutes. Discard marinade. Makes 6 to 8 servings.

Quick & easy appetizers...wrap pear slices with prosciutto or melon wedges with thinly-sliced turkey. Ready in a snap!

Pineapple & Ham Quickies

20-oz. can pineapple tidbits,   4 1/4-inch thick slices
    drained   cooked ham, cubed

Place a pineapple tidbit, a ham cube and an additional
pineapple tidbit on toothpicks. Place on an ungreased baking
sheet. Broil 3 to 4 inches from heat source for 3 to 4 minutes.
Makes about 2 dozen.

Sausage-Cheese Balls

1 lb. ground sausage   8-oz. pkg. shredded Cheddar
4 c. biscuit baking mix   cheese
                                   2 t. fresh sage, chopped

Combine all ingredients; roll into one-inch balls. Place balls on
ungreased baking sheets; bake at 350 degrees for 20 minutes.
Makes 6 to 8 dozen.

When friends visit, set out appetizers in lots of
different rooms...it encourages everyone to
move around and meet new friends.

Hot Crab Dip

3 8-oz. pkgs. cream cheese,
    cubed and softened
1/4 to 1/2 c. milk
2 6-oz. cans crabmeat,
    drained

1/2 c. green onions, chopped
1 t. prepared horseradish
1-1/2 t. Worcestershire
    sauce

Combine all ingredients in a lightly greased 3-1/2 quart slow
cooker. Cover and cook on high about 30 minutes or until
cream cheese melts, stirring occasionally. Cover and continue
to cook on high until mixture is smooth; add more milk if
necessary. Turn heat to low and continue cooking 3 to 4 hours.
Remove cover just before serving. Serve with crackers or bagel
chips. Makes about 4 cups.

Children's sand pails make whimsical ice buckets
for any seaside party!

Water Chestnut Roll-Ups

1 lb. bacon
8-oz. can whole water
   chestnuts

1/3 c. catsup
1/2 c. sugar

Cut bacon in half, widthwise; roll one piece of bacon around one whole water chestnut. Place, seam-side down, in an ungreased 13"x9" baking dish; bake at 300 degrees for one hour and drain. Combine catsup and sugar; pour over chestnuts and bake one additional hour. Remove to a serving platter; serve with a toothpick in each. Makes about 32 servings.

Celebrate the 4th of July with flags, food and fun!
A parade-day picnic with lots of yummy snacks and
frosty sodas is a terrific summertime idea.

Artichoke-Spinach Dip

14-oz. can artichoke hearts, drained and chopped
1-1/2 c. mayonnaise
1-1/2 c. grated Parmesan cheese

4-1/2 oz. can diced green chilies, drained
1 clove garlic, minced
10-oz. pkg. frozen chopped spinach, thawed

Combine first 5 ingredients; mix well. Squeeze excess moisture from spinach using a paper towel; add to mayonnaise mixture. Spread into a greased 9" round pan; bake at 350 degrees for 20 to 25 minutes. Serve with tortilla chips or crackers. Serves 6.

Serve dips and salsas in hollowed-out peppers, artichokes, bread bowls or tomato halves...no bowls to wash!

Celebration Deviled Eggs

12 eggs, hard-boiled
    and peeled
1/2 c. mayonnaise
2 T. onion, chopped
1 t. fresh chives, chopped
1 t. fresh parsley, chopped
1 t. dry mustard

1/2 t. paprika
1/2 t. dill weed
1/4 t. salt
1/4 t. pepper
1/4 t. garlic powder
milk

Cut eggs in half lengthwise and remove yolks. Place yolks in a shallow bowl and mash with a fork. Add remaining ingredients, except milk; stir well. If necessary, stir in a little milk to achieve desired consistency. Spoon yolk mixture into egg white halves. Cover and chill before serving. Makes 2 dozen.

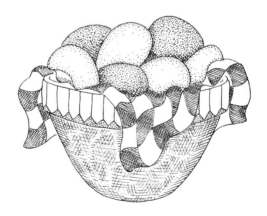

Use a pin to prick a small hole in the large end of an egg before boiling it...keeps them from cracking!

Tangy Barbecued Meatballs

2 lbs. ground beef
1 c. corn flake cereal,
    crushed
1/3 c. fresh parsley, chopped
2 eggs

2 T. soy sauce
1/4 t. pepper
1/2 t. garlic powder
1/3 c. catsup
2 T. dried, minced onion

Combine all ingredients, mixing well. Form mixture into one-inch meatballs; place in an ungreased 13"x9" baking pan. Pour sauce over meatballs; bake at 350 degrees for 45 minutes. Makes 15 servings.

Sauce:

16-oz. can cranberry sauce
12-oz. bottle chili sauce

2 T. brown sugar, packed
1 T. lemon juice

Mix all ingredients in a saucepan over medium heat. Stir until melted and smooth.

Stuffed Mushroom Caps

25 mushrooms
1 onion, chopped
1/4 c. margarine
1-1/4 c. shredded mozzarella
    cheese

3-oz. jar bacon bits
3/4 c. bread crumbs

Rinse mushrooms and pat dry. Remove stems; set caps aside. Chop stems finely; sauté stems and onion in margarine in a medium skillet. Remove from heat. Stir in cheese, bacon bits and bread crumbs, mixing well. Spoon mixture into mushroom caps. Place on ungreased baking sheets; bake at 350 degrees for 12 to 15 minutes or until lightly golden. Makes 25.

Bite-size treats always disappear fast at a potluck and are a snap to make. Simply bake a favorite quiche or cheesecake recipe in mini-muffin pans!

Slow-Cooker Nachos

1 lb. ground beef, browned
    and drained
1-lb. pkg. shredded Cheddar
    cheese
1 T. chili powder

2 t. Worcestershire sauce
14-1/2 oz. can chopped
    tomatoes
3 to 4 jalapeño peppers,
    chopped

Mix all ingredients, except chips, in a slow cooker, stirring to
combine. Cook on high for one hour; reduce heat to low for
2 hours. Serve with tortilla chips.

Taking a filled slow
cooker to a party can
be tricky, so here's a
handy tip. Slip a large
rubber band under one
handle, twist it around
the knob on the lid and
wrap under the other
handle. The lid will
stay secure!

Spicy Black Bean Salsa

8-oz. can black beans,
   drained and rinsed
2/3 c. corn relish
1/4 c. onion, minced

2 t. lime juice
1/4 t. ground cumin
hot pepper sauce to taste

Stir all ingredients together and allow to stand, covered, for 30 minutes. Serve with pita chips. Makes about 2 cups.

Crunchy Baked Pita Chips

4 rounds of pita bread

1 t. garlic powder

Split pita bread rounds; cut each round into 8 wedges. Sprinkle with garlic powder and place in a single layer on an ungreased baking sheet. Bake at 350 degrees for 10 to 12 minutes or until crisp. Store in an airtight container. Makes about 5 dozen.

No more flimsy paper plates...they'll fit nice and snug inside a Frisbee!

Onion Blossom

4 onions
2-1/2 c. all-purpose flour,
   divided
4 t. paprika
2 t. garlic powder

1/2 t. pepper
1/4 t. cayenne pepper
1/2 c. cornstarch
1 c. water
oil for deep frying

Cut off the top portion of each onion and peel away first layer
of onion skin. Make several vertical slices through onions,
being careful not to cut through the bottom of the onions.
Allow onions to sit in ice water, covered, for about 4 hours to
open. Combine 2 cups flour and spices. Dip onions in seasoned
floured mixture; shake off excess. In separate bowl, combine
remaining flour, cornstarch and water. Dip onion in second
batter; shake off excess mixture. In a deep fryer, add enough
oil to cover onion and fry each onion at 350 degrees for about
5 to 7 minutes. Makes 4.

Serve a variety of dipping sauces with an Onion
Blossom...ranch, blue cheese and dill all taste great!

Southwest Potato Skins

6 potatoes
1 lb. ground beef
1/2 c. onion, chopped
1 t. salt
1 t. pepper
1-1/4 oz. pkg. taco
   seasoning

2 12-oz. pkgs. shredded
   Cheddar cheese, divided
12-oz. pkg. shredded
   mozzarella cheese
Garnish: chives, bacon bits
   and sour cream

Bake potatoes at 450 degrees for one hour or until potatoes are tender. Cut in half lengthwise and scoop out center of each potato, leaving 1/4 inch around the edges. Save centers of potatoes for another recipe. In a large skillet, brown ground beef with onion, salt and pepper; drain. Add taco seasoning and simmer. Place potato halves in a greased 15"x12" baking dish. Sprinkle with half of Cheddar cheese and 2 tablespoons ground beef each, then top with mozzarella and remaining Cheddar cheese. Broil 3 to 4 inches from heat source until cheese is bubbly. Sprinkle on chives, bacon bits and sour cream. Makes one dozen.

Appetizer parties are a great way to visit with friends during the busy holiday season. The recipes are so quick & easy to prepare so more time can be spent catching up.

Fresh Fruit Salsa

2 apples, cored, peeled
   and diced
2 kiwi, peeled and diced
1 c. strawberries, hulled
   and sliced
1/2 c. orange juice

zest of one orange
2 T. brown sugar, packed
2 T. apple jelly
8 8-inch flour tortillas
sugar and cinnamon to taste

Combine apples, kiwi, strawberries, orange juice, zest, brown sugar and apple jelly in a mixing bowl; cover and refrigerate. Cut flour tortillas into wedges. Sprinkle sugar and cinnamon over tortillas; place on an ungreased baking sheet. Bake at 325 for 6 to 8 minutes or until golden; remove from oven and let cool. Serve with salsa. Makes 5 cups.

Creamy Vanilla Fruit Dip

1-1/2 c. buttermilk
3.4-oz. pkg. instant vanilla
   pudding mix

8-oz. container frozen
   whipped topping, thawed

Combine buttermilk and pudding mix; beat with an electric mixer for 2 minutes. Fold in whipped topping; chill 2 hours before serving. Serve with fresh fruit, gingersnaps or vanilla wafers. Makes about 3 cups.

Save the fronts of pretty seed packets and decoupage them on tiny, lead-free terra cotta pots...they make the cutest containers for holding dip!

Cucumber Sandwiches

8-oz. pkg. cream cheese,
   softened
1 c. mayonnaise
1-oz. pkg. dry Italian salad
   dressing mix

1 loaf sliced party rye bread
1 cucumber, thinly sliced
dill weed to taste

In a medium mixing bowl, blend together cream cheese, mayonnaise and dressing mix. Spread half of bread slices with cream cheese mixture and top each with a cucumber slice. Sprinkle with dill weed and top with remaining bread slices; chill until ready to serve. Makes 40 to 50 sandwiches.

Cut bread slices with cookie cutters for the prettiest
Cucumber Sandwiches!

Chicken Fingers & Honey Mustard

1/2 c. honey
1/4 c. Dijon mustard
4 boneless, skinless chicken
    breasts
1 c. all-purpose flour

1/2 t. salt
1/4 t. pepper
3/4 c. milk
oil for deep frying

Blend honey and mustard in a small bowl; set aside. Cut each chicken breast into 3 to 4 strips. Mix flour, salt and pepper in a small bowl. Dip chicken strips in milk then roll in flour mixture until well coated. Pour 1/4 inch oil into a large skillet. Heat over medium-high heat. Place chicken in a single layer in hot oil. Fry about 3 minutes on each side or until golden and crisp. Drain on paper towels. Serve with honey mustard. Makes 6 to 8 servings.

Fingers were made before forks.
-Jonathan Swift

Barbecue Cups

3/4 lb. ground beef, browned
    and drained
1/2 c. barbecue sauce
1 T. dried, minced onion
2 T. brown sugar, packed

12-oz. tube refrigerated
    biscuits
3/4 c. shredded Cheddar
    cheese

Combine ground beef, sauce, onion and sugar; mix well and set aside. Place biscuits in ungreased muffin tins; press dough along bottom and sides of muffin tins. Divide meat mixture between muffins. Sprinkle with cheese; bake at 400 degrees for 10 to 12 minutes. Makes 10 servings.

Have a fondue party! Everyone brings their favorite fondue to share...just provide the goodies for dipping.

Bread Bowl Dip

1 loaf round sourdough
   bread
2 c. mayonnaise

3 cloves garlic, minced
1 T. dry Italian dressing mix
1 c. grated Parmesan cheese

Cut a circle out of the top of the sourdough bread. Scoop out the inside, tearing into bite-sized pieces; reserve for dipping. In a medium mixing bowl, combine remaining ingredients; scoop into hollowed bread bowl. Bake at 350 degrees for one hour. Serve with bread pieces. Serves 8 to 10.

A tasty gift...share several favorite dip recipes and add a set of old-fashioned ramekins.

Cheddar Fondue

1/4 c. butter	1/4 t. Worcestershire sauce
1/4 c. all-purpose flour	1-1/2 c. milk
1/2 t. salt	8-oz. pkg. Cheddar cheese,
1/4 t. pepper	grated
1/4 t. mustard	

Melt butter in a saucepan; whisk in flour, salt, pepper, mustard and Worcestershire sauce until smooth. Gradually add milk; boil for 2 minutes or until thickened. Reduce heat; add cheese, stirring until melted. Transfer to fondue pot or slow cooker to keep warm. Serve with bread cubes or pretzel sticks. Makes 2-1/2 cups.

Appetizers in less than 10 minutes! Toss 4 lemon halves in a stockpot of boiling water and add a pound of shrimp. Cook until they turn pink, 5 to 10 minutes, then peel and eat. Don't forget the cocktail sauce!

Turkey & Black Bean Quesadillas

15-oz. can black beans,
   rinsed and drained
6 oz. Cheddar cheese, cubed
12 slices cooked turkey, cut
   into strips

1/2 c. salsa
8 8-inch flour tortillas
2 T. butter, melted
Garnish: sour cream and
   salsa

In a large mixing bowl, stir together beans, cheese, turkey and salsa. Brush one side of tortillas with butter. Place buttered-side down on an ungreased baking sheet. Spoon about 1/3 cup filling on half of each tortilla; fold in half. Bake at 375 degrees for 10 to 15 minutes or until heated through; let cool 5 minutes. Cut each quesadilla into 3 wedges. Garnish with sour cream and salsa. Makes 24 servings.

Looking for a new way to serve a favorite snack?
Retro-style plates, cake stands and bowls
really add color and fun.

Bacon-Cheddar Puffs

1/2 c. milk
2 T. margarine
1/2 c. all-purpose flour
2 eggs
1/2 c. shredded Cheddar
    cheese

4 slices bacon, crisply
    cooked and crumbled
1/4 c. green onion, chopped
1/4 t. garlic salt
1/4 t. pepper

Bring milk and margarine to a boil over medium heat. Add flour, stirring until mixture forms a ball. Remove from heat and add eggs, one at a time; blend until smooth. Add cheese, bacon, green onion, garlic salt and pepper; mix well. Drop by teaspoonfuls on greased baking sheets. Bake at 350 degrees for 5 to 8 minutes. Makes 3 dozen.

For a fun relish tray, make onion curls! Cut the stems of green onions into lots of thin slices, soak in ice water and soon the ends will begin to curl.

Roast Beef Wraps

1 c. sour cream
2 T. prepared horseradish
1 T. Dijon mustard
5 8-inch flour tortillas
30 spinach leaves, stems
   removed

10 slices cooked roast beef
1 c. shredded Cheddar
   cheese

Combine sour cream, horseradish and mustard; blend until creamy. Spread mixture equally on each tortilla and layer on several spinach leaves. Place 2 slices roast beef over spinach; sprinkle cheese on top. Fold opposite edges of tortilla toward the center, over the filling, then begin rolling one of the open ends toward the opposite edges, rolling tightly. Refrigerate 2 hours. Before serving, slice each wrap into 2-inch pieces. Makes 6 to 8 servings.

When mailing invitations, send along a blank recipe card asking guests to bring copies of their appetizer recipe to share....someone's sure to ask.

Spinach Pinwheels

8-oz. pkg. cream cheese,
  softened
1/2 c. sour cream
1/2 c. mayonnaise
1-oz. pkg. ranch dip mix
3-oz. jar bacon bits

4 green onions, chopped
2 10-oz. pkgs. frozen
  chopped spinach, thawed
  and drained
10 8-inch flour tortillas

In a medium mixing bowl, combine cream cheese with sour
cream and mayonnaise. Add dry dip mix and stir to combine.
Add bacon bits, onions and spinach; mix well. Spread mix on
tortillas to within 1/2 inch of edge and roll up tightly. Wrap
each tortilla in plastic wrap and chill overnight. Unwrap and
cut each into one-inch slices. Makes 6 dozen.

Try using flavored wraps instead of tortillas for
roll-ups...sundried tomato-basil, garlic-herb or cilantro
really give them a zippy new taste.

BLT Dip

1 lb. bacon, crisply cooked
   and crumbled
1 c. mayonnaise

1 c. sour cream
2 tomatoes, chopped

In a medium serving bowl, blend together bacon, mayonnaise and sour cream. Fold in tomatoes just before serving. Serve with tortilla chips or fresh vegetables. Makes 2-1/2 cups.

Parmesan Spread

8-oz. pkg. cream cheese,
   softened
1/3 c. grated Parmesan
   cheese

1/4 c. mayonnaise
1 t. dried oregano
1/4 t. garlic powder

Blend ingredients together in a medium mixing bowl; cover and chill at least one hour before serving. Serve with bagel chips or crackers. Makes 1-1/2 cups.

Triple Cheese Ball

2 8-oz. pkgs. cream cheese, softened
8-oz. pkg. sharp Cheddar cheese, grated
8-oz. pkg. crumbled blue cheese
1/2 onion, diced
1-1/2 T. Worcestershire sauce
2 T. red pepper flakes
1-1/2 c. finely chopped pecans, divided
1-1/2 c. fresh parsley, chopped and divided

Blend together cheeses, onion, Worcestershire sauce and red pepper flakes; mix in one cup pecans and 1/2 cup parsley. Cover and chill one hour. Shape into 4 balls. Combine remaining pecans and parsley; roll balls in mixture. Cover and chill until ready to serve. Serve with crackers or crispy baguette rounds. Makes 32 servings.

Give extra taste to recipes with cream cheese by trying one that's flavored...chive, garlic and sun-dried tomato are all so yummy!

You're invited

to an

appetizer party!

where ....

when ....

what to
bring ....

rsvp ....

Star-spangled flag designators
are a snap to make! Just copy,
cut out and secure to a
toothpick with a piece
of tape.

Celebration
Deviled Eggs

from the kitchen of: _____

_____

_____

_____

_____

_____

_____

_____

Spicy Black Bean Salsa

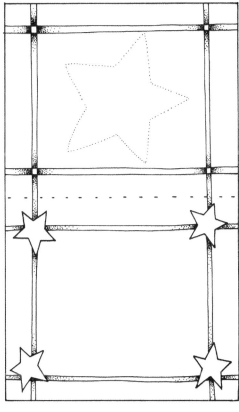

Someone's sure to ask, so jot down your recipe on a copy of our handy recipe card. And if you write the recipe name on a table tent, everyone will know what goodies you've brought! Just copy, cut, fold in half and set alongside your dish.

Index

Artichoke-Spinach Dip..................................10
Bacon-Cheddar Puffs....................................25
Barbecue Cups..21
BLT Dip..28
Bread Bowl Dip...22
Celebration Deviled Eggs.............................11
Cheddar Fondue..23
Chicken Fingers & Honey Mustard..................20
Creamy Vanilla Fruit Dip..............................18
Crescent Chicken Bites...................................5
Crunchy Baked Pita Chips.............................15
Cucumber Sandwiches..................................19
Fresh Fruit Salsa..18
Hot Crab Dip..8
Jalapeño Poppers..2
Onion Blossom..16
Oven-Toasted Potato Chips.............................3
Parmesan Spread...28
Pineapple & Ham Quickies..............................7
Roast Beef Wraps...26
Sausage-Cheese Balls.....................................7
Slow-Cooker Nachos....................................14
Sour Cream-Ham Dip.....................................3
South Street Tortilla Roll-Ups..........................4
Southwest Potato Skins.................................17
Spicy Black Bean Salsa..................................15
Spinach Pinwheels.......................................27
Stuffed Mushroom Caps................................13
Tangy Barbecued Meatballs...........................12
Triple Cheese Ball..29
Tropical Chicken Wings...................................6
Turkey & Black Bean Quesadillas....................24
Water Chestnut Roll-Ups.................................9